Manipula
and Mind Control

How to Recognize Deceptions,
Stop Be Manipulated and Be Free
to Live a Successful Life

Written By

Abraham Goleman

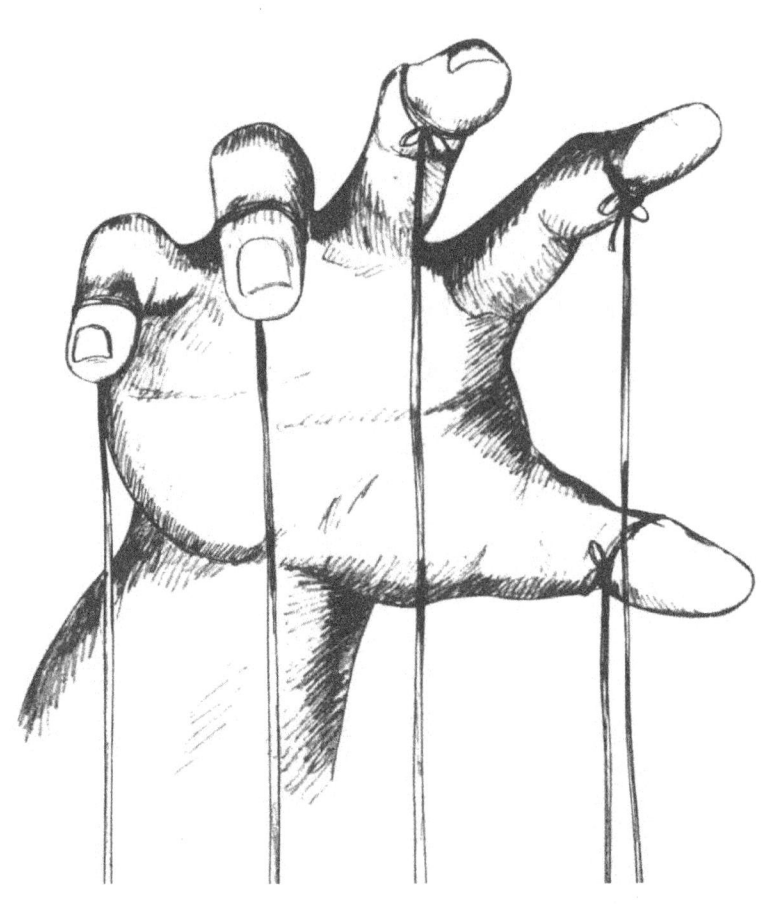

© **Copyright 2021 - All rights reserved.**

The content contained within this book may not be reproduced, duplicated or transmitted without direct written permission from the author or the publisher. Under no circumstances will any blame or legal responsibility be held against the publisher, or author, for any damages, reparation, or monetary loss due to the information contained within this book. Either directly or indirectly.

Legal Notice:

This book is copyright protected. This book is only for personal use. You cannot amend, distribute, sell, use, quote or paraphrase any part, or the content within this book, without the consent of the author or publisher.

Disclaimer Notice:

Please note the information contained within this document is for educational and entertainment purposes only. All effort has been executed to present accurate, up to date, and reliable, complete information. No warranties of any kind are declared or implied. Readers acknowledge that the author is not engaging in the rendering of legal, financial, medical or professional advice. The content within this book has been derived from various sources. Please consult a licensed professional before attempting any techniques outlined in this book.

By reading this document, the reader agrees that under no circumstances is the author responsible for any losses, direct or indirect, which are incurred as a result of the use of information contained within this document, including, but not limited to, — errors, omissions, or inaccuracies.

Table of Contents

INTRODUCTION 7

Understanding Deception 8

    Dark or Not? 8

    The Deception Spectrum 10

    Signs of Deception 12

    Tips used in spotting a liar. 17

Detecting Lying and Deception 22

Manipulation Is Not Evil; It's Just A Tool 28

    What Is Manipulation? 28

    The Qualities of A Manipulative Person 33

Master Your Emotion is The Key 38

    What Is Emotional Influence? 39

    Principles of Emotional Influence 41

    How to Recognize and Overcome Negative Emotions That Control Your Life 49

Indoctrination Strategies 68

    How Can You Influence Others? 72

Brainwashing 79

The Conscious Level 81

The Unconscious or Behavioral Psychology................................. 82

Biological Psychology 85

Hypnotic Induction 87

What Are the Differences Between Hypnosis on Stage And In Real Life?...91

What Are the Advantages of Hypnotizing Someone?................... 95

Techniques of Dark Psychology 97

The Door in The Face! 98

Foot in The Door 99

"Yes-Set" Technique 101

Linguistic Presupposition 103

Reverse Psychology 104

Negative Hidden Commands 107

CONCLUSION 109

INTRODUCTION

Thank you for purchasing this book!

This handbook will look at the role of manipulation within the workplace and the family setting. The phenomena explore how people deceive others and coerce them into doing their bidding. After reading through this book, you will learn more about the traits possessed by malicious individuals

Enjoy your reading!

Understanding Deception

Dark or Not?

Deception is a critical part of dim brain research. In the same way as other dim mental strategies, it very well may be hard to tell if any given case of trickiness is dim. Before we investigate the distinction between dull and typical trickiness, we should initially see precisely what duplicity is.

Many individuals would express the perspective that lying and trickiness are something very similar. This is mistaken. Lying is a type of trickery; however, it is in no way, shape, or forms the main structure duplicity can take. Instead of considering double-dealing "lies," it is smarter to consider it "misdirecting." Any activity or word equipped for causing somebody to think some different option from reality can be precisely named trickery.

So, what are some basic signs of trickiness? Lying, excluding reality, inferring misrepresentation, or deceitfully giving proof to something bogus are largely tricky instances. You will likely understand that you have done a portion of these things, eventually yourself. Does that imply that all demonstrations of duplicity are instances of dull brain research? Not in any way.

Everybody tricks somewhat or another. Individuals may trick others for a scope of reasons, for example, consideration, humiliation, or sentiments of insufficiency. For instance, contemplates have demonstrated that many men will lie about their stature on dating sites. This doesn't make them experts of dull brain science! Individuals even fool themselves about the scope of issues, including their wellbeing, aspiration, and satisfaction. Such everyday instances of duplicity don't compare to dim trickery.

Trickiness can be viewed as dim when done with either an adverse or detached expectation toward the hoodwinked individual. Powerlessness generally propels typical trickery to look up to reality somehow. Then again, Dim duplicity agrees that reality doesn't serve the tricky points of the double-crosser. Hence, the fact of the matter is either changed, covered up, or overlooked for a rendition of occasions that better suits the motivation behind the individual misdirection.

Set forth plainly, individuals who send dim brain research use duplicity to hurt, not assistance. They help their advantages, however, at any cost, paying little heed to who gets injured.

A few people accept that if duplicity is the little scope, it can't be viewed as dull, while bigger double-dealings must be inalienably dim. This isn't the situation. By investigating the possibility of the double-dealing range, you will see that it isn't the duplicity size that decides if it is dull or not, rather the reason behind the trickiness.

The Deception Spectrum

To comprehend the possibility of misdirection, comprehend that it can happen on either an enormous or a small scope. One of the principles messes up that individuals frequently expect that trickiness is just genuine if it is huge and doesn't make a difference if it is little. This is a grave mistake. Little duplicities can be utilized in an intensely dim manner by gifted controllers and are regularly more viable than enormous trickeries. The absolute biggest double-dealings ever are done by purposeful controllers to serve their points and goals. Dull instances of different kinds of misdirection, huge and little, will currently be introduced to outline the possibility of the trickery range.

So, what is a portion of the manners in which more modest trickeries can be utilized by individuals who practice the craft of dim brain research? Regularly, little misdirections are utilized to test the casualty's naïveté and condition them into accepting the controller's beguiling explanations and activities. If individuals are molded to accept a scope of more modest lies after some time, they are bound to accept a bigger lie later on. This progressive molding isn't the main way more modest trickeries can be utilized as a dull mental weapon.

More modest double-dealings can likewise be completed to sabotage a casualty's trust in their forces of rationale and reason. Suppose a controller tricks a casualty over minor issues, and the casualty starts to address what's going on. In that case, the casualty may well presume that their doubt is silly, and they consequently can't confide in their judgment. Many people are bound to infer that their judgment is defective, as opposed to someone else is misleading them over minor issues. Clients of dim brain science know about this general "trust" that individuals have and misuse it without leniency.

Enormous scope trickery can likewise be an illustration of dim brain research, practically speaking. Perhaps the biggest trickiness conceivable is to persuade somebody that you are an unexpected individual compared to what you say you are. Not regarding the character or some other detail. A whole personality. Name, date of birth, everything! The most talented clients of dim brain research can convince others to purchase totally into their depiction of a bogus personality and foundation.

Since it has been demonstrated how manipulative clients of dull brain science can utilize the trickery range for their points, we will probably investigate the most well-known themes, and subjects' individuals are bamboozled about. At that point, we will take a gander at precisely how these huge and little scope duplicities are completed by investigating the particular strategies that are utilized.

Signs of Deception

Deception is similar to lying, but it has some different components. One of them is equivocation. Equivocation is when someone makes vague or ambiguous statements. The point is to make things unclear, not to point out the mistake in their logic. Deception is making things seem a certain way when they are not that way. Deception is when a person uses any tactics to help make a situation seem different than it is. Lying by omission is one example of this. Lying by omission is when a person leaves out important information for the sake of changing others' perception of reality. Deception is done without a person's knowledge. It changes their perception of the situation without actually lying. Camouflage is another example of this deception technique. This happens when someone is trying to hide the truth to realize that they are missing some of the story's necessary parts. This will be used when someone is employing half-truths. Camouflage will happen when somebody is trying to hide their real name or what they do for work. Camouflaging can be conceptualized as a way to hide in plain sight, in metaphorical terms. A skilled person in employing camouflage will change their entire persona, including body language, when necessary.

One unique, more specific strategy often used in Dark Persuasion is the "give and take." The give and take technique works by fitting you into a dialogue about whatever the subject matter at hand is. The "give and take" technique works because a trick people into thinking that they are actually in an equal relationship when they are not. People tend to trust those with whom they engage in a back-and-forth. They start to think that they are in an honest relationship because there is a feedback loop. This is often not the case. One way to do this is to ask for someone to do a small favor for you. Once they have done the small favor, you then require that they do something else for you. Once both of these are completed, you pay them back. This might be by doing a small favor for them. It might be by offering some kind of material response, like money. Money is one of the biggest motivators for humans living in our time. Now, by establishing this loop of the give and take, you have established a relationship.

Deception, alongside fraud, confusion, imagination, misleading, and beguilement, is a show used to spread emotions in the subject about contortions or almost the whole way feelings. Deception can consolidate a collection of things, such as disguise, spread, impedance, capable deception, presentation, and dissimulation. The director will decide to control the subject's cerebrum, considering how the subject will trust them. The subject will recognize what the ace is communicating and may even be basing reachable plans. Forming their reality depends on what the expert has been letting them know.

On the off chance that the master is rehearsing the deception methodology, they tell the subject will be counterfeit. Trust can, without a considerable amount of a stretch, be pummeled once the subject discovers, which is the clarification the ace must be gifted at the technique of deception and exceptional at getting something moving if they need to proceed with their subject.

Typically, deception will develop the degree that affiliations can incite sentiments of vulnerability and unfaithfulness between the two partners in the relationship. This is considering how deception hurts the rules of most affiliations and is in like way observed to impact the needs that go with that relationship. A considerable number of people need to choose to have a real discussion with their embellishment; if they have discovered that their partner is surprising, they would need to understand how to use confusion and impedance to get the solid and reasonable data that they need. In some way, the trust would be gone from the relationship, making it difficult to develop the relationship back to where it had once been. The subject would dependably be exploring what the ace was outlining for them, thinking about whether the story was authentic, or something made up. Because of this new vulnerability, most affiliations will end once the subject finds a couple of arrangements concerning the master's deception.

Some of the signs of deception are:

The Lack of Self-Reference

If a person is truthful, they will utilize the pronoun "I" when describing what took place. For example, an honest person will go ahead and say, "I arrived home and went straight to the bedroom. After that, I went to talk to my mother, and we had a lengthy chat." That's just an example statement. As we can see, the pronoun "I" appears twice in the statement provided.

Deceptive people will use language that minimizes the number of "I" references. During an oral statement, the witness or suspect may leave out some important information; this can happen even when issuing an informal written statement.

Answering A Question with A Question

Even though a person may be a liar, they will prefer not to engage in the act of lying. When a person lies, they risk being detected. Before you answer a question with a lie, you should avoid answering the question at all costs. When trying to act dodgy, people may often answer a question with another question. The investigators should always be on the lookout for people that answer a question with another question.

Tips used in spotting a liar.

Focus on Building Rapport

It is evident that a "good cop" will always display better results than a "bad cop." During an interview, a person may appear as empathetic, and they will gain access to more information than the person who appears cold. It is also advisable to avoid being accusatory during the interrogation process.

Surprising the Suspects

A deceptive individual will always try to anticipate your next move after a move. For instance, they may try to anticipate your question so that they can ensure each answer they are issuing seems natural. You should always ask those questions that they do not expect.

Listening More Than You Speak

If you are a liar, you will focus on speaking more, and your main goal is to ensure that you will sound legitimate. Also, you will focus on winning over a certain target audience. Some liars may make use of some complex sentences so that they can conceal the truth.

You should be aware of the following things:

When people are stressed, they tend to speak faster.

A stressed person will speak louder.

The liars usually clear their voice and cough regularly, which means that they are experiencing some tension.

Although the statements that have been mentioned above are supposed to enlighten you on how to spot a liar, it is good to note that some people may exhibit some signs of tension, but that is not an indicator that they are lying to you. In case you have noticed any of the mentioned actions, you should proceed with caution.

Pay Attention to How A Person Says "No"

When engaging a suspect, you should pay close attention to how they utter the word "No." A person depicting some unusual behavior will always face another direction as they say, "No." They may also appear hesitant, and they can also close their eyes.

Watch for The Changes in Behavior

When a person changes their behavior, it is an indicator that they may be engaging in deceptive behavior. You should be careful when a person issues some short answers to different questions. Also, they may pretend that they are suffering from memory lapse, especially in a critical moment. They can also start to speak formally, and they may start issuing some exaggerated responses.

Always Ask for The Story Backward

If a person is indeed truthful, they will add some details. They will focus on remembering more stories about what happened. A liar will start by memorizing the story, and they will stick to one narrative. If they add some details, you will notice that they are not adding up by taking a close look at the details. If you suspect someone is deceptive, you should ask them to recall the event in a backward manner, rather than issuing the narrative from the beginning to the end. You can ask them to talk more about what happened right before a certain point. A person who is telling the truth will usually recall many details. A liar will simplify the story, and they will also contradict themselves.

Beware of The Compliments Issued by People

Although compliments are good, they are only good if a genuine person has issued them. You should always be on the lookout for a person who is trying to make a good impression. When you agree with all the opinions being issued by a person and also laugh at all their jokes, it is an indicator that you may be insincere.

Asking A Follow-Up Question

People do not like dealing with liars; however, it is good to remember that sometimes people are uneasy with some questions since they avoid personal embarrassment. Also, some people may be extremely dependent on the outcome of a specific conversation.

For instance, during a job interview, a person may be tempted to hide the details about why they may have been fired from their past job. Although the person may be qualified and their personality is good, they may hide some of these details since they need a job. During the interview, a person may issue a response that may seem puzzling. If you are puzzled during an interview by some of the responses, you can develop some follow-up questions. If you are in doubt, you can continue to ask questions. With time, you will be able to spot whether a person is deceptive or not.

Detecting Lying and Deception

There are signals that we send only in a certain situation. If you only knew what your subconscious mind is doing this would be easier ascertained. But before that, we will deal with another interesting problem: what happens to our subconscious when we try to lie.

A person who claims to be able to read minds and analyze others should notice when they lie to him. You have already learned to recognize the signs of falsehood and to guess from the face, whether a person is lying or telling the truth. But the most difficult thing you have to master is to see when people lie with their whole bodies.

The easiest way to lie is in words. We do this throughout our lives. It is harder to lie using facial expressions, although many people also do it well. But the most difficult thing is to lie with your whole being (or body). We do not think about it, but the body has its own language and often says what it wants, and not what we intended. In conversation, people pay attention primarily to words, less often to facial expressions and almost never to the body of the interlocutor.

When we suspect a person of lying, we carefully listen to his words, instead of paying attention to the tone of his voice or body language. But this is the only way to check whether a person is lying or not. In fact, we see the signals of the excitement that he is experiencing (and when he lies too). He may be nervous, not because he is lying, but for another reason. There are signals that mean a lie and only a lie—and we need to learn to distinguish.

Some people are well versed in lies and its various manifestations. Others circle the finger easy. There are congenital liars for whom lying is like breathing. They do not send any signals and usually as referred to as psychopaths. There are also people who do not know how to lie. We are all different. But most of us send signals that can be distinguished.

The ability to recognize lies has always been admired by people. Without this skill, it is difficult to work in the police or in court. The testimony of the classic "lie detector" is sometimes erroneous, so many scientists, including Paul Ekman, spent so much time and effort to learn to recognize a lie, and in part, they succeeded. But first, let's think about what a lie is.

Most people lie all the time, or rather, their words do not quite accurately reflect reality. This is how our society and culture are organized, where lies are accepted. To the question "How are you?" The person answers "Good," he does not talk about his problems, because the other person is not interested in the interlocutor and in fact, he is just being polite.

There are situations when people are forced to lie and hide their thoughts. At a beauty contest, the winner may sob from excitement, while the losing participants are forced to smile and pretend to be happy for her. If a lie was not accepted in our society, the participants of the beauty contest would sob bitterly and possibly would have pulled the finalist by the hair. When you do not show your true feelings—this is a kind of lie.

Of course, these forms of lies do not interest us. We are interested in when people lie not out of politeness or on sociocultural motives, but on their own initiative — consciously, knowing that things that do not correspond to reality. Remember, lies are not only the lies that we speak but also the truth about which we are silent. If I say that I won a tennis match, which I actually lost, then I lie. If I say that I am having fun, but in fact I am sad, I lie.

When someone lies, he does it out of fear of punishment or in the hope of reward. Our lies always have a reason. There is also a combination of these two motives: when we want to receive an undeserved reward, but if a lie is revealed, a fine is waiting for us. For example, everyone will know that we have lied—this is also a punishment to some extent.

Conflicting Signals

A person gives false signals only when the reason becomes a very significant factor or when a person risks something when he is worried. And it is the excitement that is reflected on his face—the feeling that we can read as a sign of lies. First, you need to find all the signals, and then correctly interpret them. In the case of a lie, there are always two messages: truthful and deceitful, both equally important, we must learn to distinguish between them. The message comes not only from our words but also from the whole body—all the tools that combine under the name "nonverbal communication" are used. Therefore, we are talking about how skillfully a person hides a truthful message and gives a lie instead of the truth. It is about self-control (that is, control over emotions and reactions). As is the case with the meaning of a facial expression, a person tries to disguise one feeling with another. To understand whether he is lying or not, you need to follow the channels of communication that are the most difficult to control. A person who speaks the truth unconsciously sends similar signals, but if we feel a symbolic discrepancy between words and facial expressions of a person or movements of his hands, then we can talk about lies. This is what I mean by "conflicting signals." We say one thing, think the other, and do the third. And the easiest way, of course, is to control your words.

Manipulation Is Not Evil; It's Just A Tool

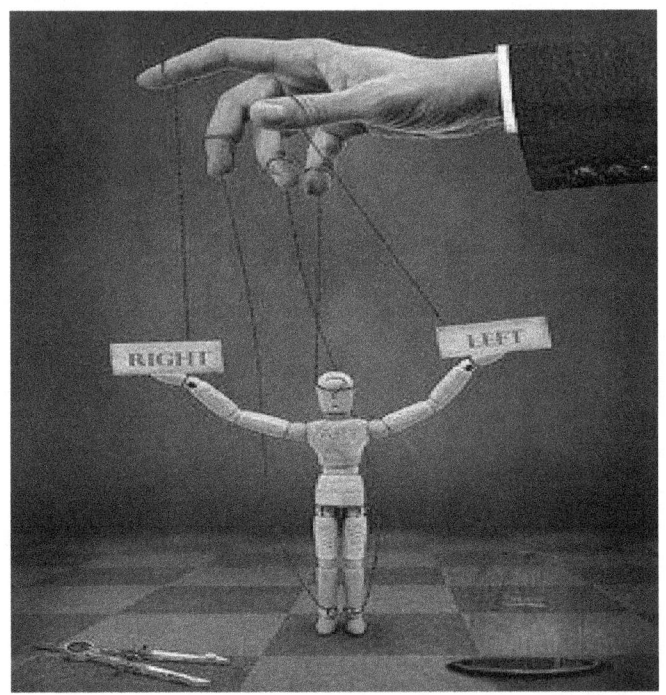

What Is Manipulation?

A speedy check of your word reference would give various meanings of control. In this field, control is depicted as a type of social impact that targets changing the recognitions or practices of different gatherings ordinarily through misleading, injurious, or naughty techniques. All in all, the controller is continually seeking after their inclinations at the person's expense in question. In that capacity, the vast majority of the methodologies they utilize are exploitative, harsh, underhanded, and tricky. Social impact isn't unsafe. However, when the methodology utilized prompts control, it may cause negative results.

When a specialist convinces a customer to change their way of life to defeat medical problems, such as heftiness, we can allude to this social impact. This is an innocuous illustration of the impact. The equivalent applies to all different types of impact whereby the individual is doing the affecting means well for the receptor on the most fundamental level. In actuality, if an individual uses a type of pressure to get their direction and advantage from the receptor's activity or response, this is viewed as a destructive impact and will buy a large amount to control.

Dull enthusiastic or mental control has a few parts of intimidation and influence in it. The parts of intimidation are many, however genuine models incorporate conditioning and tormenting. From a human outlook, these two are beguiling and injurious. The individuals who use control comprehend this excessively well, yet they need to utilize them to impact their casualties. Before the control starts, the controller normally has its ultimate objective in their mind. What remains is to examine the expected casualties and afterward choose the best types of maltreatment to apply in constraining them to achieve them. Coercion is a typical methodology utilized in such occurrences.

A survivor of control may not intentionally cling to the requests of the oppressor. Notwithstanding, they may come up short on any other options, compelling them to allow them their will, contingent upon the strategy used to impact them. Manipulative individuals regularly show an absence of affectability and care towards others; thus, they don't see anything amiss with their activities. An alternate sort of controller just thinks about their ultimate objective and is uninterested in who they hurt in the end route, be it a kid, relative, or dear companion. Most manipulative individuals maintain a strategic distance from solid connections since they dread not being acknowledged. On the off chance that such an individual gets into a relationship, they can't assume responsibility for their issues, practices, and life all in all. What follows is they start the cycle of control and make their accomplices assume control over those obligations.

On the off chance that you examined all types of psyche control, you would understand that a controller can utilize a large portion of them to pick up the impact they frantically need. One of the most widely recognized strategies over the five sorts of psyche control is an enthusiastic shakedown. Here, a controller thinks of an arrangement to summon blame or compassion from their casualty. They see all around very well that blame and compassion are among the most grounded human feelings, which will probably open up their objectives to their control. When their gatekeeper is dropped, the controller exploits the subject and starts the compulsion cycle. Quickly, the subject of control winds up coordinating and helping the regulator in achieving their evil objectives.

One danger of manipulators is that they are not only good at evoking these emotions, but they can evoke them in immeasurable degrees in comparison to the situation at hand. Such a person will make a small situation such as being late to work appear to be as huge as causing a whole company's collapse.

Emotional blackmail is one of many tactics employed by manipulative people. There are others, such as a covert form of abuse known as crazy-making. Just like the name suggests, the manipulator aims to make their subject feel crazy. They create a scenario where the victim develops self-doubt. At times, the self-doubt level might be so severe that the subject might think they are losing their mind. There is yet another form of manipulation where the manipulator acts as if to verbally support their victim but give non-verbal cues that portray contradicting meanings. If they get confronted, they revert to rationalization, justification, deception, and denial to escape trouble.

Another big problem with manipulators is that they might not always be aware of what their subjects need. At times, they might be aware of them but cannot consider and provide them. This does not, at all, justify their behavior. What it does is show that a manipulator will neither consider nor prioritize these needs. They also do not feel any pity, guilt, or shame. The dangerous thing about this trait is that it makes it hard for the manipulator to stop their harmful influence. If this is a point to consider, it explains why some victims of this vice never realize the extent of the damage until it is too late.

Manipulators are also solitary humans. They are most likely to be found alone because they never form or sustain long-lasting relationships. The problem is that after forming relationships of any form, their manipulative nature creeps in and scares their friends or lovers away. People who relate with manipulators confess to feeling used and lacking trust towards the controllers. In this case, the problem affects both parties; first, the controller will not recognize or provide the other party's needs. On the other hand, the affected person will not succeed in creating the emotional connection required to sustain the relations. In the end, both parties go their way, and the manipulator is once again left alone.

The Qualities of A Manipulative Person

According to George Simon, a psychology writer, there are distinct qualities that define a manipulative person. If someone possesses these traits, their chances of being successful manipulators are extremely high. Similarly, if one lacks these traits, they cannot use other people to attain their selfish goals. I bet this is one of those qualifications we all do not want!

In Simon's words, a successful manipulator must:

- Have the ability to hide their aggressive nature and intentions from the public, and more so their potential targets.

- Have the ability to identify the vulnerable aspects of their potential victims to decide which approach to use for efficient manipulation.

- Have an extraordinary level of brutality, which enables them to overcome the qualms that might arise from the harm they cause to their subjects. Ruthlessness can be emotional or physical.

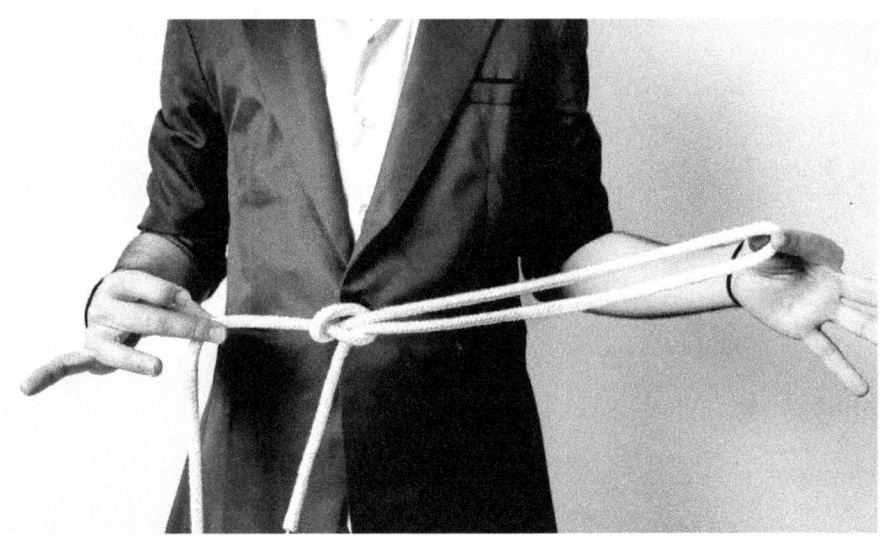

As we can see, the first trait that a manipulator needs to influence other people successfully is the ability to cover up their aggressive intentions and behaviors. Imagine if they went around talking about their dark secrets and plans, nobody would dare to befriend them for fear of being manipulated. The manipulator develops a camouflage that hides their thoughts and plans from other people, ending up appearing normal. Often, the victim walks into the trap with the least suspicion and might not realize it initially. The oppressor will come off as a Good Samaritan, a best friend, or a random person acting sweet. By the time the target becomes suspicious, the manipulator already has enough information to coerce them as they please successfully.

After, the controller must have the skill to observe and determine the vulnerable traits of their victims. This is a typical proverb application that if you must cut down a tree, you better take your time to sharpen your ax. From the identified weak points, they can sit down and decide on the best approach to eating them and effectively attaining their goals. At times, the manipulator will use observation to identify the vulnerabilities, while in others, they need to interact with their subjects for a certain period.

The final trait is that cruelty must be applied. It would be pointless for the manipulator to put in the work required in the above steps to start worrying about what their victims will feel or what will happen to them. If they cared about anyone at all, they would not come up with these plans in the first place. That said, the manipulator puts all the care behind them and ignores any emotional or physical harm that may occur to the victim. To them, what matters is that they achieve their end goals.

From these three traits, we can tell why manipulators succeed most of the time. The amount of planning and trickery that they use is bound to catch anyone off-guard. Due to this, the subject will not be quick to realize that they are in the middle of a manipulative process until the effects begin to show up. They might assume that the oppressor wishes them well, making them drop all defenses. By the time they come to their senses and want to get out, they are already stuck.

Master Your Emotion is The Key

Many people pride themselves on being rational creatures—after all, humans frequently justify their superiority through rationality, even if that rationality is negligible at best. They like to think that they make decisions based solely upon rationality. However, that cannot be further from the truth.

Do you remember when emotions were mentioned and how they are major motivators for humans? Those same emotions can be tapped into to create the results desired by others. People can frequently be swayed to do certain things or act in certain ways through emotional influence.

What Is Emotional Influence?

Emotional influence refers to the process by which people and corporations appeal to your emotions to sway you to do something. Perhaps most commonly seen in marketing practices, it works off of the idea that the part of the brain that regulates emotions is also related to decision-making. This makes sense—if emotions are meant to help someone make decisions that will make the individual more likely to survive, it makes sense that the same part of the brain is responsible for processing thoughts.

The way this works is with the theory that the brain works off of dual processing. This means that your brain has two systems that enable it to function—system one, unconscious, meaning it is automatic, nearly instant, and low effort, and system two, which is conscious, meaning it is controlled and takes more effort and is slower.

With the principle of dual processing in mind, you can see that emotions would be regulated by system one while system two would involve rationality and logical decision-making. Between the two, system one, your emotional regulatory area, is always running, which also implies that you are far more likely to make instant, emotional reactions simply because that process is already running in the background of your mind and it requires very little effort or time. Essentially, system one will kick in, make a gut reaction, and then system two will slowly

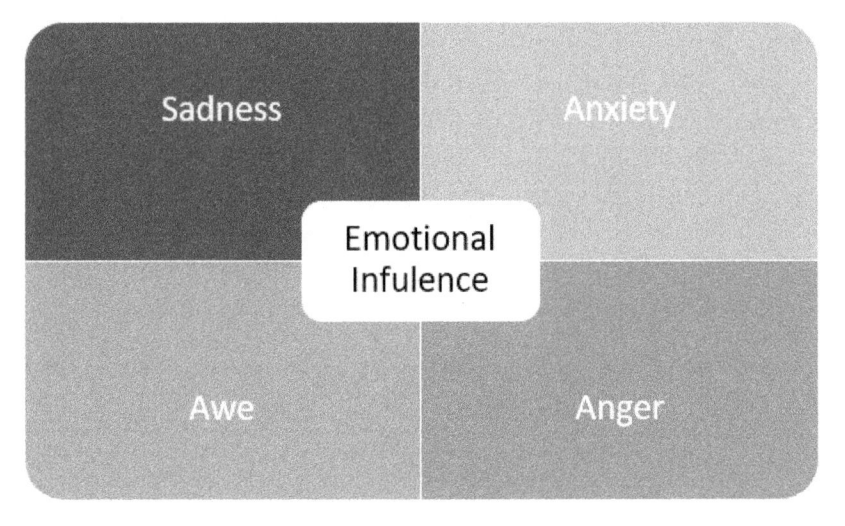

Sadness	Anxiety
Awe	Anger

Emotional Infulence

rationalize that decision.

Think about two brands that have been largely seen as rival competitors, where people usually pick a favorite and run with it. It could be whether you are using Apple or Microsoft on your computer, or even whether you prefer cats over dogs. If you are asked which you prefer, you will likely answer one or the other without thinking about it reflexively. This is your emotional system at work. System two, on the other hand, would then kick in, and you would be able to offer the reasoning for that decision.

We think this idea with our emotions first, and rationality following can be particularly useful, especially in dark psychology. If you can appeal to emotion, you can sway the rational side of the brain. If their emotions naturally guide people, you are far more likely to get the results you want if you can sway them one way or another.

Principles of Emotional Influence

When looking at emotional influence, four major motivators will sway the decision-making process. All emotions sway decision-making to some degree, but ultimately, these four emotions are the most persuasive. Sadness, anxiety, awe, and anger are the most motivating in terms of inspiring action. You may notice that three of the four are negative—and that is intentional. Negative emotions inspire actions that are meant to avoid them in the future. You want to make the negative emotions stop, and frequently, you may be able to get a reprieve from the emotion based on the decisions you make. For example, sadness can be mitigated temporarily by doing something that you feel stops the cause of the sadness in the first place.

Sadness

Remember—sadness or sorrow is essentially emotional pain. It involves loss, pain, harm, disappointment, or helplessness and implies a need for support and time to heal. It is a negative influencer—it makes you act in ways that will help you avoid feeling sad for that reason again.

Sadness impacts the brain by making the brain function slower. If you are sad, your brain is essentially fogged—have you ever heard the expression "brain fog?" It is felt when sad. The sadness can be overwhelming, acting as a blanket over the person's mental processes and makes decision-making more difficult.

Despite this brain fog, however, people tend to make decisions based on short-term benefits. They want to achieve happiness as quickly and easily as possible, and they will make poor long-term decisions simply to avoid further pain of sadness. They are more likely to undervalue both their actual worth and the worth of other items, as evidenced by people's tendency to price items and services lower when feeling sad than when feeling neutral or happy.

All of this culminates in someone likely to behave impulsively in ways that they think will assuage their sadness. Think of commercials that are meant to make you sad to get you to donate money. They may claim that you are only donating less than a dollar a day, never mind the fact that even offering up $0.50 a day is still going to add up to $182.5 over a single year. While $0.50 in a donation may seem negligible at best, it adds up over time, culminating in a much larger donation over a year that people might hesitate to give in one lump sum. People are more likely to donate those pennies to that sad ad because they want to make the sadness stop, and they feel that offering up the donation would be enough to make it happen.

Awe

Awe is a state of wonder, typically reserved for things that are seen as more powerful or greater than an individual. Typically, people are left in awe of the vast expanse of space, the depth of the ocean, the mystery and daunting task of assembling Stonehenge, or when viewing other similar objects or meeting people that are influential and seen as superior.

When something or someone leaves you in awe, you are more likely to focus on what is happening at the moment. You will feel more aware of what is going on around you but less aware of the passing time. You are in that moment without regard for time, and that focus allows you to appreciate whatever is happening at the moment. This presence at the moment consequently makes people more willing to give. People will be more likely to help others when in awe and are more likely to make decisions that will be more generous than if they felt anxious or afraid.

This is important—you can usually convince someone to do something by first impressing them with something glorious. Think of marriage proposals. For example, they are frequently done with big gestures, such as taking someone on a trip to somewhere breathtaking before proposing. There is a reason for this; people are more receptive when they are in awe. If you take your partner somewhere to propose and you can trigger that awe, you are more likely to get the yes you are looking for.

Anxiety

Anxiety goes hand-in-hand with fear. It is typically an emotion that is felt when anticipating a negative result of something and often is joined by nervous behaviors. For example, if you feel anxious about getting into a car accident, you may have a deep-seated fear of dread every time you enter a car or have a sense that you will die if you get into the car.

When attempting to decide, people who are actively anxious will struggle to read the situation accurately. They will fail to identify cues or context around them, such as recognizing that someone is attempting to manipulate or persuade them to do something that will not benefit the long run. Because anxiety is associated with nervousness, people tend to struggle to identify whether they are in a situation that is stable or that will change shortly, so they struggle.

When feeling anxious, people are particularly receptive to persuasion, and they are far more likely to second-guess their impulses or reactions. It has been found that 90% of those who are actively feeling anxious in the moment are likely to seek advice from other people, whereas only 72% of people are willing to do the same in a neutral emotional state.

Lastly, when feeling anxious, you are more inclined to behave selfishly, simply because you are in survival mode. People in the throes of anxiety are often far more concerned with their feelings than with how others may potentially see them, and because of that, they make decisions that will solve their problems with little regard for the long-term consequences.

Appealing to someone's anxiety can also create fantastic results when attempting to persuade them. Think of a salesperson who wants to sell a newer model car to get a larger commission—she might appeal to the other person's anxiety, emphasizing all of the safety features of the newer model and telling a story about someone who got into an accident in the car that the person is looking at and how the accident did not end well at all. Particularly when used against parents, who only want the best for their children, this can sway people to make decisions that they believe will keep them safer because it helps soothe their anxiety. At the moment, feeling anxious and imagining their children being hurt in the other car, the people are more likely to make the impulsive decision to buy the more expensive, newer car model, even if it is a poor long-term decision.

Anger

Anger is incredibly intense. It spurs you to respond to things aggressively and is often used to protect boundaries that are being perceived as being challenged or violated. It allows you to protect those boundaries, cueing for you to protect yourself in the process. Ultimately, anger is incredibly motivating because of self-preservation instincts.

When angry, people are more successful at recognizing arguments that are weak or strong. They feel more in control and see where things are wrong or weak than strong, compelling arguments. Angry people feel a call to action—they think that something must be changed, and they will work to achieve it. Think of some of the most major social reform that has been accomplished—it is usually around societal issues that instill anger in seeking the change. The people involved were able to clearly and convincingly articulate themselves, which enabled them to make sure the change they wanted to have occurred.

Ultimately, anger can be used to motivate change for that very reason. Suppose people feel as though they have had their rights infringed upon or that something is inherently wrong. In that case, they are more likely to respond with anger, which, in moderation, becomes the most efficient of the emotions in terms of persuading someone to act.

How to Recognize and Overcome Negative Emotions That Control Your Life

We agree that negative emotions are the emotions that make you miserable and sad; the kind that causes you to dislike yourself and other people, taking away your confidence. Depending on the manner you choose to express them and the length of time you allow them to affect you, these negative emotions will dampen the enthusiasm you have for life.

Negative emotions will also keep you from behaving and thinking rationally, from seeing situations through a clear, unbiased lens. When this happens, you see things the way your mind wishes to interpret them, and you remember only what your mind wants to remember. This is a flawed way of viewing and experiencing life because it keeps you from dealing with reality, and the problem with this view of life is that it only prolongs your frustration, anger, and disappointment. Also, the longer you hold on to false beliefs, the more entrenched the prevailing issue will get. On that account, failure to deal with your negative emotions appropriately is harmful.

Recognizing Negative Emotions

The first step to dealing with negative emotions is to recognize and to decode them. To decode an emotion is to slow the emotion or thought process involved, as though you had hit the slow mode on a remote, so that you watch the process frame by frame, systematically, until you find meaning in what is happening.

Most times, when people realize that they are having negative reactions towards other people or a situation, they are often quick to take up measures to reverse their reaction. For example, a wife might say to you, "Tell me what to do to stop being so angry at my husband." Another might say, "What should I do to increase my confidence when speaking in front of a crowd?" From these two popular statements, the people are looking for solutions rather than getting to the root of the problem to understand what could be causing anxiety or fear when speaking in public and what could be the root of the anger felt towards the husband. The reality is that emotions are at the root of all thoughts and actions you take.

The first step towards dealing with the negative situation is to identify the negative emotion that lies underneath. Identifying the actual feeling will provide you with incredible insight into why you are acting the way you do, and therefore allow you to approach the same situation from a different perspective. The principle here is that for you to understand clearly, what you are dealing with, you must first identify the driving emotion.

Below is a step-by-step tactic to help identify and decode your emotions:

Identify the Trigger Thought or Event

Think back to what was crossing your mind when you started feeling as you do right now. It may take a minute to roll back the tape as far back as you can remember. What do you find therein that could have caused your negative emotions? There was likely an event or something that happened to you, something you saw, or an interaction you had with someone that dampened your mood.

From there, now think about the mental response you gave to what happened. Could you have thought that the situation is never going to improve, you are not good enough, you will never succeed, you always take the blame, or that you have had enough? Whatever statement rushed into your mind, take note of it and write it down. Once you have done that, it's time to proceed to step two.

The Emotion or Reaction You Gave

What feeling went with the thought or reaction you gave? Identify the emotions you are having. Is it anger, frustration, fear, loneliness, or pain? (Think along the lines of the emotions we listed in the previous chapter). From the list of emotions, you might identify one or two of those. Write those down, and you can proceed to the third step.

Identify the Physical Manifestation of Your Emotion

What are you feeling in your body, or how is your body reacting to your emotions? Are your fists clenched? Does your face feel hot? Do you have stiffness in your neck or a headache? Is there pain in your stomach? Well, the physical manifestation varies from one person to the other, and there are no wrong answers here. Only take your time to identify how your body may have changed.

Besides, you are learning a new skill, and it requires patience and full attention. Once you have identified the said sensation, put it down on paper also.

By now, you have a 'chain' of events listing the negative thought, the emotion you felt, and the reaction or sensation that followed. Let's see an example:

"I am the only one who seems to care" --- Loneliness, Frustration, anxiety --- Headache, Hot Face

Look at what you just did. You unraveled the reason behind your negative emotions. You can correctly identify how you are feeling (lonely, anxious, and frustrated), you know how it is manifesting in your body (a hot face and a headache), and you know the reason why this is happening (people have left you to do something by yourself). You finally have an idea about how your mind works when driven by negative emotions.

Before having this information, how would you have to behave instead of what you are feeling? Chances are you wouldn't have taken time to even determine the feelings running through you. Sometimes, people confuse anxiety, fear, disappointment, and frustration with anger. You would have probably taken up action to fight anger while you were just anxious. You would have behaved in the wrong manner too. However, you now have a vivid description of your emotions and your trigger.

With the information above, will you react differently from how you would have behaved, typically? Do you think you can now make different choices with the information you have got now? The goal of taking time to identify the negative emotions is to slow down your reaction time so that you have enough time to process your mind. That way, your body will give a different reaction.

For example, once you identify the negative thought underlying, your next task is to challenge your thoughts through positive talk and reality testing. For example, you could ask yourself, "Do I complain every time I am asked to do a task by myself?" "Do people react negatively whenever I speak to them?" "Do I patiently request for assistance when I perceive a task as too great for me to do by myself?" or "Am I just a nice and cool person that people keep misconceiving?" The chances are that the answers to questions like these will calm you down and keep you from overreacting.

As for the emotions you have taken note of, the process is not about rushing to solve or numb them; sometimes, you only need to recognize them for what they are. After that, all you have to do is take caution and take care of yourself whenever the emotions arise. For example, whenever you feel alone and fearful, ask a friend to come by, and if at work and you feel like you have been left to handle a difficult task by yourself, ask for some help until when you are comfortable enough to take on the role by yourself. If you have felt angry because of something that was done to you, find a productive way to utilize the extra energy, and diffuse the anger.

Identifying the physical reaction and from where it manifests is important because it allows you to learn how to cope with your emotions and the consequent physical responses before the thoughts and feelings you have to fester or grow into something bigger and unmanageable. As you practice doing this and keenly listening to your body even when you do not have any negative emotions, you will realize that your body gives forth so many messages. These messages are often masked in unhealthy coping habits like shopping, drinking, unhealthy coping, eating, and oversleeping, among others.

For the most part, your mind will be influenced by the state of your body, and when you are unaware of the condition your body is in, you will not understand the feelings, thoughts, and judgments that you come up with. However, as you become better at identifying the physical location of your feelings, you will be able to connect with the respective emotions also. Once you do that, you will start taking measures to take care of your body better, and this could be as simple as taking more breaths, taking deeper breaths, and some stretching to get rid of the physical tension.

Identifying your emotions is the first step to behavioral change, and your thoughts and physical reactions have everything to do with it. When you have control of your emotions, thoughts, and actions, you have control over the influence negative events will have on you. Try to practice the exercise given above as often as you can, and if you are willing to be more vulnerable, you could do it along with your partner, friend, or family member. Discuss with them the various reactions you exhibit because they may have noted a behavioral response you had not given any thought to.

Whichever approach you take up, the point of doing this exercise is to increase or enhance awareness of your emotions and to advance your thought process so you can learn more advanced strategies and patterns to slow and manage your reactions.

As you learn how to manage stressful situations in this new way, compare your progress with how good you did when you did not know this three-step process. See how you have grown and progressed. You will be proud of the person you have become.

Overcoming Negative Emotions

People take up various approaches to overcome their negative emotions. Some opt for diversions, others distractions while others choose to bury the negative emotions, only to realize that they did not move past the feelings they were having, and are still stuck in their negativity. The struggle to move past the negative influences while still being pulled back by the unresolved issues will feel like an internal battle. However, it is possible to overcome negative emotions in the right way.

Research and personal experience will tell you that struggling with, trying to drown out, arguing with, and pushing out the emotions you have only amplifies them and makes them worse. Therefore, as you go through the following steps, keep in mind that there are no quick fixes, and it will take patience, practice, and persistence on your part to achieve the intended goal.

Steps to Take to Overcome Negative Emotions:

Walk away from any negative thought patterns

Patterns are typically repetitive, which means that negative thought patterns allow negative, unhelpful thoughts to repeat themselves. As you would expect, this process yields negative, unpleasant, and unwanted emotions like depression, fear, anxiety, shame, unworthiness, and stress. As such, the key to avoiding negative thoughts is to cut out the negative thought patterns in the first place.

The process of walking back from negative thoughts is called cognitive defusion. Cognitive defusion encourages you to learn to see your thoughts simply as that, like thoughts. You see, when we join our thoughts to our persons, we end up taking the thoughts very seriously, and we believe them, even when they are not true. However, the cognitive defusion state demands that you do not take your thoughts too seriously; you only hold them lightly.

While taking your thoughts very lightly, you only take notice of them when they seem valuable and helpful. In doing this, you should remember that not all your thoughts will be 'truthful' or valuable, which means that you shouldn't follow through or play out each of them. Think of those thoughts as bits of information that pass through the mind every now and then, and you have a choice in how you choose to deal with and respond to each thought.

Let's consider this example: suppose it's on your wedding day and in the morning, you look out the window, and it's raining. What would be the first thought that would rush through your mind when you see the rain? You will think that your day is now ruined. You might say, "What a dreadful day it's going to be." If you think about it, does rain cause an entire day to be ruined? Of course not. Rain is just like any other weather. However, if you go by the thought that the day will be dreadful, you will be stuck in cognitive fusion because that negative thought will have fused with your thoughts, and guess what will await you? A dreadful wedding day. This is to show that whenever you allow your negative thoughts to take control, you are only aiding in the process of generating negativity, to your detriment.

In explaining cognitive defusion, I do not assume that negative thoughts will not come up. They will because they are a part of our daily lives. It is not every day that your life will feel like a fried egg, sunny-side up! Negative thoughts will come up. The problem, however, is not the negative thoughts, but your belief that the thoughts are true. Whenever you disentangle yourself from this kind of negativity, the unpleasant thoughts lose their power and the ability to generate negative emotions.

Now, getting back to our example, suppose that on the morning of your wedding, you looked through the window and saw that it was raining. The negative thought: "what a dreadful day," came up and you only allowed it to float around in your mind, without buying into it. As you continue watching the rain, you also start to see the negative thoughts fall away. In this case, when the thought came up, you did not believe it, did not fuse with it, and did not allow it to generate any emotions in you. Instead, you slide back into a chair or lie on your bed and begin to think how lovely the day will be. You start to rehearse your vows, and you imagine living with the love of your life. All this as the pitter-patter of the rain continues on the roof.

The second scenario shows just how much easier it would be to avoid negative emotions after recognizing unhelpful thoughts. Stepping back can be extremely liberating, and it can change the quality of your day or even your entire life.

Become Aware

From your experiences, you must have noticed that your negative thoughts flow from two distinct directions: dwelling on issues of the past and worrying about what is to be in the future. When you dwell on the past, you mostly ruminate over mistakes, guilt, problems, and issues in the past that did not go as you had hoped they would. On the other hand, people worry about the future because they are afraid of what might or might not happen in the future, for themselves and others.

Negative thoughts, particularly about the future, are common. People worry that they might not achieve particular goals or have anxiety because of their relationships or finances. Others worry that their skins are aging. Others worry that they are not doing as well as their peers. Whatever the negative thoughts of worry are, you will notice that for them to turn into anything substantial, your mind must have been engaging with thoughts of the future or thoughts about the present. For example, if you think your current job is too difficult or underpaying, you are likely to be worried about the future, that you may not be able to sustain your family with the money you are getting. While that may push some people to do something about their current financial situations, most people do not get past the point of worrying.

When you are lost in negative thinking, you become so engrossed in them that you lose touch with what is currently going on in your life. The result is that you miss out on the little joys of today. Have you watched a movie where a spouse was so engrossed in the other's mistake that he or she did not notice the good that his or her partner was doing, and eventually, the accused partner grew tired and walked out of the relationship? You must have. That is how we miss out on the good about the present focusing on the past that we cannot change or the future that we cannot predict. In the end, we end up losing 'partners.'

Instead of obsessing about things, take time to enjoy the sunshine today. Do you feel the taste of the food you are eating? Are you taking time to enjoy the relationships you have with your friends and loved ones? Have you thought about what is good today? Did you notice the sunshine, or the drops of rain falling? There is so much beauty around you; you cannot afford to get lost in your head and lose touch with the world around you or lose touch with who you are.

The way to step out of any negative thinking is to 'come to your senses.' This means that you need to redirect your attention from the thoughts that run through your head and instead, focusing on what your sense perceives presently. Wherever you are, whether in the park, on the subway, at home, or in your office, take some time to notice all that is around you. Engage all your senses, and don't be tempted to involve your mind and start a mental dialogue as you do this. Your goal here is to only be aware of what surrounds you. When you do this, you will be practicing mindfulness. Slowly, your mind and your senses will calm down, be grounded, and be fully aware of your surroundings.

Practice Mindfulness Daily

As we grow and become more taken by our problems, desires, hopes, goals, and dreams, we forget the deep, inborn peace and pure unconditioned inborn awareness that is entrenched deeply in all of us. In this state, it is easy to be so drawn into your negative thoughts that you lose your sense of self.

In reality, your mind is like an ocean on which surface waves will cause great tumult on the surface, yet the depths remain unaffected and peaceful. Inside you perfect stillness, just beneath your thoughts, habits, and conditioning which tend to be tumultuous. Beneath all that is an undeniable quiet that serves as a calm refuge, and it is always available for you.

As such, mindfulness is the ability to get down to that natural wellspring of peace and wholeness. It is the ability to get out of your wondering state so that you can live consciously. Mindfulness allows you to live with that inner peace, to the point that you can gain a deeper awareness and monitor your mind. The result is that you will have decreased stress, anxiety, and depression. It also improves the working of your immune system.

People who practice mindfulness report greater life satisfaction and happiness while those who allow their minds to wander lead unhappy lives.

Distinguishing Helpful from Unhelpful Thoughts

Getting rid of some negative thoughts can be quite difficult, resisting both the identification and the mindfulness approach. If you are in a situation like this, and you discover that some thoughts are 'sticky,' there remains an approach you can take to untangle yourself from your thoughts. This approach involves asking yourself some helpful questions to challenge unhelpful thoughts and redirect your focus.

Some of the questions you should give some answers to include:

Is the thought helpful or unhelpful?

If yes, am I sure that it is helpful?

Are these thoughts coming up out of habit?

Do your thoughts make you take some effective action?

The questions above will help you determine whether your thought ought to be left alone to die or whether you should attend to it. Once this is done, you should now focus on the questions below to see if you can find a new focus or some new possibilities. These questions will help you shift to some creative actions and thoughts and enable you to face daily challenges more effectively so you can have a more meaningful life.

They include:

What is the underlying truth in this situation? Where do I truly stand on this issue?

How do I expect the situation to play out, and how can I work towards that?

How best should I handle this situation?

How would my life play out if these negative thoughts did not come up?

How can I see this situation from a different angle?

What new thought or story should I now focus on?

How much more can I be grateful for the moment and my surroundings?

Once you answer the questions above, you will be on the path to changing your focus from being stuck in negativity to focusing on what is going well. This way, you can also take on constructive action and make your life more meaningful.

Indoctrination Strategies

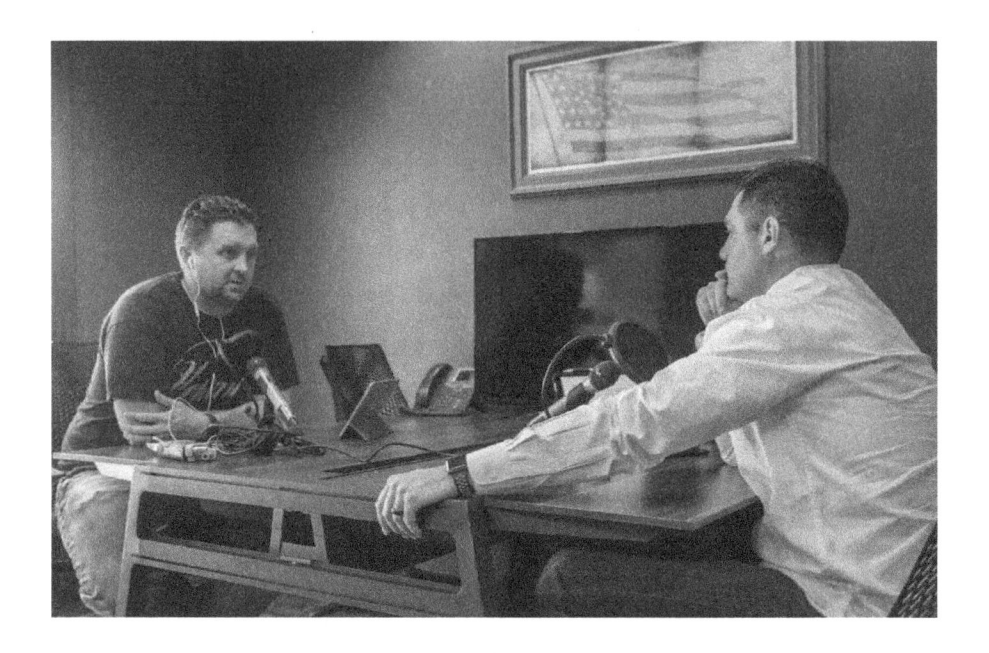

As you read familiar words, be aware of what they intend and disguise. Uncover this content in front of you and others. Before you take words in essential matters, check to see if those words fit your goals. Words can prevent or facilitate proper knowledge of the problem.

Do not recklessly accept other people's words but try to express your ideas in your own words. Do not take on the problems or the alternatives of your opponents but formulate yourself the problem or the alternatives. Check what and with which words are you regularly sprinkled or indoctrinated. Which messages do you always hear, who is trying to keep your attention in constant control? To what extent have you already come to terms with someone else's ideas? For example, did you notice that in the spring of 2007, a car manufacturer rented 80 percent of all billboards in Germany and Switzerland for several weeks to publicize a new car model? Maybe even three years following, you can remember which model that was.

Make a regular game of scrutinizing the advertising that you encounter critically for their actual information content. Distinguish between information and sentiment. Also, think about which external influences you can entirely or partially escape. Autonomy means self-determination and, as a prerequisite, also requires distance, rest, and time with oneself.

Often advertising with popular spots is targeted at children. When they then lurk advertisements all day long, they become tools of subtle indoctrination. This is particularly effective in making it even harder for children to turn off than watching TV.

The fact that in most private broadcasters, the most exciting films are interrupted abruptly, especially in the most dramatic moments by a suddenly breaking advertising message, is not only a disgrace for the spectator, but also aims at the very moments in which one with the largest internal openness sits in front of the screen. You can protect yourself and your children against such psychoterrorism by providing targeted broadcasters without advertising or DVDs.

In his article The One-Dimensional Man, social philosopher Herbert Marcuse wrote that people in modern society had lost sight of alternatives. You would usually only see and recognize one side of things. This is the one associated with the familiar or dominant word creations.

This process is a prerequisite for opinion dictatorship, for one-sidedness and lack of tolerance. In order not to become so one-dimensional yourself, you should always strive for alternative thinking. Everyone knows that everything has two sides, but who lives by that principle? Open accordingly for counter positions or views that are foreign to you or that you would reject. If you try to get involved, you will most likely discover meaningful aspects of the truth in it.

Try to break out of conventional thinking and to think differently about situations or situations. Develop alternative problem solving or life designs. Imagine a few castles in the air or plan your election campaign and design a concept of your world politics. Think about what might be wrong in the right direction and what could be recommended in the forbidden.

Think across! At least mentally break out of your usual horizons again and again. Our company, your company, you are good at alternatives, goals, dreams, and visions. They are the sources of new and meaningful developments.

To find out what has influenced you so much, you should, with some distance, once again clarify the persons, circumstances, milieus, scenes, and groups you coined, as well as the family, the party, and Worldview in which you grew up. If you wonder which motive and interest you have been doing so manipulated in, you may be able to think of clearing out some of them more clearly and working out your own identity and your own will.

You may also wonder how your preferences match those of the groups you currently belong to. The greater the correspondence you see in detail, the more likely you assume that your thinking is foreign. Then think about the points you differ from the group opinion and try to communicate that as well. The resistance you encounter will make you realize how convinced the group is.

In principle, you should also consult and weigh up other opinions and positions before making your own opinion on an important issue.

The so-called climatic catastrophe does not seem to threaten as much as it has been propagated in the media over a longer period. It would be better to a possible Climate change, and its currently still unpredictable consequences of speaking.

If you find yourself constantly in agreement with many other people's opinions, you should become restless. Maybe you are over-adjusted. In many cases, education amounts to making one flexible and adaptable. The less one's own identity is formed, the less opinionated and stubborn one becomes, the easier it is to follow instructions and commands. Children were brought up to follow. If this becomes a life principle beyond puberty, the pedagogically desirable goal of maturing is not achieved. Being mature means having your own opinion and being able to say it.

Trust your judgment more than anyone else. Have the courage to express your opinion even where you have to expect contradictions and do it wisely and kindly.

How Can You Influence Others?

How far you can influence the consciousness of groups or society depends, in part, on your position and the attentiveness to that position. The more public attention you have, the further your impact will be.

Influences can also be created artificially. Groups, businesses, individuals are doing public relations to get known. This is trying to attract attention. If that does not succeed in the positive, then if necessary, also in the negative. The main thing is to get attention, get in the public perception, and remain in the conversation. Methods to gain attention are:

- Leaving the conventions

- Breaking the rules of normalcy

- Do something extraordinary

- Violated expectations

- Do something crazy

- Provoke by taboos

- Making noise and causing a stir

You can build a positive image by associating yourself or your name with perceptions, feelings, objects, or attitudes that create positive emotions in other people. Also, by strengthening others' self-esteem through recognition, praise, or compliments, you can elicit positive feelings from them. These are most likely to be returned to you.

Once you have ranked high, anything you say following will have a higher recognition value. Your confirmation will make you appear as a well-meaning ally whose expertise will not be called into question for a moment. Depending on how you need it, you can add a positive or negative color to your words. One way of upgrading is to substitute one word for another, positive one:

- Preserved thickened milk mucus from the can for the Coffee is sold as a lucky clover.

- A journal becomes the essence of the latest findings.

- A health insurance company becomes a health insurance fund.

- It is not a pair of jeans which are sold, but a sexy butt.

- Another way to add value is to add a positive adjective or epithet to nouns:

- Lunch becomes a delicious meal or a culinary delight.

- Politics becomes a forward-looking peace policy.

- A written report becomes a comprehensive report or - with the substitution of the noun - a concise conclusion.

- A birthday party becomes a funny birthday party or even a special event for a friend.

In the devaluation, one proceeds analogously and plot terms negatively:

- From the delicious birthday cake, it becomes one fat calorie bomb.

- The five-star hotel becomes a bonze shed.

- The luxury sedan becomes a pimp sleigh.

- The street musician becomes a noisy beggar.

In this way, you can try to make things appear in the light you want to show them. It greatly increases the likelihood that your message will arrive as you wish.

Enemy images are negative ways of identifying oneself from which one delimits oneself. Whoever declares anyone or anything to be the cause of all evil and at the same time conveys to the addressee the feeling that they have nothing in common with this cause of all evil can easily expose himself as the savior from ruin and pull the people to his side:

Firstly, if the Taliban and Al Qaeda are evil and try to expand, you can consider yourself good because you are not one or the other. Secondly, you must become active to do something about evil. After all, one cannot allow his expansion to be inactive. If someone tells you what to do about it, you can hardly say anything against it. They would eventually recognize themselves as sympathizers of the wicked.

A Chancellor is often called a Chancellor of the Peace. This name does not miss its effect. He also assumes that a possible counter-candidate is not a peace chancellor by claiming this title for himself. Simple models are the easiest to implement; they do not require thinking. Therefore, it is effective to reduce complicated issues to simple formulas.

The slogan " War on Terrorism " probably drew so much because most citizens used the term " terrorism." Thus, the war is finally as undesirable. Still, necessary minor evil in the fight against the larger accepted and considered justified.

Keywords should be so simple and clear that they remain present in every consciousness and activate a reasonably clear association field:

- The slightly different restaurant

- China in the Olympic fever

- Juppies (young urban professional people)

- Dinks (double income, no kids)

- Generation Golf

Appealing to and building on similarities makes it easier for you to be heard and, on that basis, to continue to pursue your true concern. So, you can pick up people at a joint meeting point and take them to your destination.

Constant repetition makes the alleged confidant more familiar and, therefore, more credible. This applies to the propaganda for wars in the present just as it did in antiquity: The older one, Cato, is said to have been in the Roman Senate for several years. Every one of his speeches begins with the phrase: By the way, I favor the motion that Carthage must be destroyed. He reached his goal indeed: It came to the Third Punic War, and Carthage was destroyed.

A question mark is like a hook on which something always gets stuck! Questions are apt to dispel suspicions and rumors:

- Is Mr. X cheating on his wife? Or
- Minister Y transferred the embezzlement of taxpayers' money?
- Why does Uncle deny abuse of his niece?

The language includes a rich and ingenious repertoire of possibilities to achieve and to move considerably. Depending on the intentions and interests of a speaker, this can result in great dangers, including people's disempowerment and the initiation of wars. In the service of a selfish and power-hungry manipulator, the power and magic of language can become a curse.

On the other hand, whoever wants to serve a good cause will be less successful if he tries naively to speak as his beak has grown for him. He can only effectively fulfill his request if he has as many registers in his language as possible and knows how to use them virtuoso.

Brainwashing

Brainwashing is a tactic that we often hear. We are told that television commercials bombard us with what to buy, and we are exposed to people's rants on television, radio, the newspaper, online, and social media. These rants tell us what we should look like, what we should be eating, reading, voting for, wearing, etc. We are all subjected to the art of brainwashing daily, and the amount of brainwashing continues to grow.

Before the creation of social media, we were still exposed to social media. However, they would only market to their target audience. If they weren't meant for you, they would be ignored until the after commercial or show came back on the air. For example, you wouldn't have paid much attention to a Polly Pocket or Barbie commercial unless you were a ten-year-old girl or someone who might buy the product for their child.

But things are not like that anymore. Advertising has moved past gender roles, and with the inception of social media, advertisements are now personally geared for us. These websites take information that we provide them. For instance, Facebook uses our likes, comments, status updates, etc., to find the perfect things to advertise. They are utilizing brainwashing techniques in the 21st century.

Today, we are bombarded with mind control techniques daily. There are many different types and levels of mind control. We will go over an overview of the types, and we'll talk about some examples of them. There are three basic levels of mind control. Each level corresponds with a different type of psychology. So far, no technology can control what you choose to believe. So we will talk about the methods to defend it, and we will also look at some of the implications it has on civilizations. Mind control skills are used wrong for obvious reasons, whether it's politically or scientifically speaking. Simply by existing in a society, we are constantly subject to manipulation or indoctrination.

The first-level appeals to consciousness. The second level corresponds to unconsciousness, and the last level appeals to biological. Now in terms of psychology, the first one, consciousness, has to do with cognitive psychology.

Cognitive means being aware of what's going on. The second one is unconsciousness, which corresponds with behavioral psychology and while the last one is biological psychology, which talks about psychiatry. This is where you can try to control the mind using physical things like drugs and electrical shock. Every mind control technique fits into its methods. Some of the mind-control techniques will fit into one of these levels, while some mind techniques will fit in between two of them. But every mind control technique fits inside the sun part of the chart. Now let us talk about the different levels of my control and what fits in between.

The Conscious Level

The first level is the conscious level. This level is the level that deals with information. It does not talk about punishment or physical pain. It appeals to your reason. The basic forms of this are education and ideological indoctrination.

A good example of this is when you get your driver's license. You decide to take fighting classes, and you learn the rules of the road, and the intention is to make you behave a certain way when you are driving. Now, most people don't have a problem with this because if you don't behave a certain way when you drive, you will have a problem.

So ideological indoctrination is the worldview and philosophy, and what you're educated in, in your worldview. So, this includes your political choice, education, religious education, and even your science education. Now this means how do you view the world and by what you were dictated by. Now, at this level, you have to mention the fact, which means information. Now because propaganda has been abused in the past, people normally have a negative view of it.

Now the basic idea is that somebody wants you to view the world differently, so they educate you. Propaganda is just information control. Now information control isn't that bad. For instance, have you ever seen a billboard that says that 50000 people die when driving and drinking? Now that is propaganda, and it is not bad. Hitler used propaganda to educate Germany into the idea that all Germany's problem was because of the Jews. Now that is bad propaganda.

The Unconscious or Behavioral Psychology

Now let's look at the after level of mind control, which is unconscious or behavioral psychology. This does not appeal to the Conscious mind. It is an attempt to control somebody without his or her conscious decision being involved. The biggest school of psychology is behavioral psychology that comes from Pablo psychology. A great example of that is the story of the man who rings the bell for the dog to salivate that we talked about above. So this deals with stimulus-response. Stimulus means when something happens – in the man and the dog case, it's ringing the bell. Response - in the man and the dog case, is the dog's drooling. Now, this does not appear to be a conscious mind. The dog did not decide to salivate; they just did it automatically. Now, unlike the Conscious level, this level often includes physical pain, punishment, and torment.

For instance, you can implant a commanding chip in somebody so that when they hear the command, which is the stimulus, they will go and do something, which is the response. It is a stimulus-response. The person that is programmed to do that thing doesn't decide to do it because it is an automatic response, and in fact, he doesn't even know that he is being programmed because that thing is in the subconscious. At this point, we have hypnosis, and the reason it's so is that hypnosis is implanted into the subconscious.

For instance, the operator says: when I say bubble gum, bark like a dog. So, the stimulus is the bubblegum, whereas the response is the barking like a dog. Or the operator says: when I snap my fingers, you should act like a stripper. So, he snaps his fingers, which is the stimulus, and acting like a stripper is the response. Creating a stimulus-response mechanism is called conditioning. Part of the conditioning is programming somebody to associate pain or pleasure with something. Now another part of this level is called punishment. Punishment is an attempt to make somebody associate pain with undesirable behavior.

Now let's go with: if you have a kid and the kid flicks the switch off. Now on the Conscious level, you could sit your child down and explain why it is wrong, and hopefully, your child would decide not to do it again. Now on the unconscious level, you can beat the hell out of the child until the child tends to associate pain with switching the switch off and hope and hope that doesn't do it again.

Behaviorism attempts to control somebody's behavior, like how you train a dog using rewards and punishments. Now the cognitive approach is the best, and this is the level where we have brainwashing or interrogation. And you will do this using physical pain to control someone. Another note about brainwashing is that it has the word washing, which means wipe something away and wash it away. The word brainwashing comes from a technique that was used in China, which is called political re-education. The idea is that when you want to wash something away, you put something else in its place.

In the MK-ultra program, the psychiatrist called it de-patterning. Now when you take somebody from their religion and use mind control techniques, you will be able to wipe out their religious beliefs and put another belief in his place. This is called programming. So under brainwashing, we have political re-education, we have the patterning, and we also have religious education or de-programming.

Biological Psychology

Now the last level is Biology, which equates to biological psychology or psychiatrist. Now at this level, you are attempting to control someone's behavior through physical interventions. Physical interventions include brain surgery, drugs, electrical shock, or implanting something into the brain. Now for the child who flipped the switch off, the cognitive approach will be sitting the child down and explaining why it is wrong now. The behavioral approach will be to spank him, and the biological approach will be to give him a psychotic drug. Or a remote-control robot. Now those are the basic levels. Many different mind control techniques fit into these levels, but we will not be going deep into them.

There are different levels to control somebody's behavior between the Conscious and unconscious levels, and we are constantly subjected to this daily. One of these techniques is public relations, and it is aimed to make you feel a certain way about something. Now, this is not to just make you feel good about something. It can make you feel bad about a competitor, a group, or a person. And it is called Black public relations. Now another mind control technique is marketing and advertising. Another mind control technique that falls between the Conscious and unconscious level of mind control is pandering, and the word pandering means to fulfill a moral desire, a prostitute pandering to a sexual desire, a drug dealer pandering to an addiction.

So, what this means is that you're controlling someone by giving them what they want. Under pandering, future control by destruction is included, including television, pornography, and video games. And another mind-control technique on the biological level is addiction. Manipulative people keep their victims to them by making them addicted to drugs. And beyond that, there is a reason why caffeine has been added to soft drinks, and there is a reason why energy has been added to fast food, and there is a reason why sugar is added to almost everything in the grocery store; it's because it is a type of mind control.

Now the last technique, which is at the very bottom, is when you give up on trying to control the person's mind and restrain them. An example is a straightjacket, institutionalization, imprisonment, and heavy tranquilizer. If everything fails and you can't control the person's mind, there is still something left to shoot the person. So that is basically what dark psychology brainwashing is all about.

Hypnotic Induction

Hypnosis is a characteristic perspective. It is a state given to us for personal development. There has never been an archived instance of mischief coming to anybody from trance induction's therapeutic utilization is additionally a great sentiment of complete physical and mental unwinding. It is like that second between realizing you are wakeful and going into the rest state.

An individual may decide to remain in spellbinding after an accomplished subliminal specialist requests that they emerge from it. The explanation being, it is quite a casual sentiment of happiness; they want to remain mesmerized for a spell longer. The individual at that point rests and stirs, of course. In self-entrancing, you have full oversight and set your time limit. There has never been a recorded instance of somebody incapable of emerging from spellbinding.

Nobody is mesmerized without wanting to. The hypnotherapist just helps the subject, who mesmerizes himself. Procedures exist by which one can accomplish a condition of self-entrancing and increase total unwinding under the most unpleasant conditions. In this expression, the psyche mind is available to restorative proposals.

When mesmerized, members in a phase show find that their minds become unfathomably incredible. They are glad to do foolish things for a group of people since it is simple to envision and acknowledge the trance specialist's recommendations.

In self-spellbinding, you pick your time limits, understanding that you have a decision and would now be able to choose your region for personal growth. Utilizing spellbinding toward the start of your mindfulness, preparing is of extraordinary advantage. It speeds up the retraining cycle.

Hypnosis is a perspective in which an individual's activities and feelings are controlled through a system of exercises known as spellbinding incitement. The incitement factor can shift from individual to individual and starting with one hypothesis then onto the next. Entrancing relies upon the individual's psychological situation; likewise, the individual who is delivering the upgrade.

Hypnosis has for some time been a topic of conversation and opponent speculations. A portion of the specialists has asserted that spellbinding is a sort of phony medication given to a patient as a strong one. Sometimes, just by expecting the inactive pill's impact, positive changes have been seen in the patients. These specialists accept that spellbinding is a serious type of impact. Then again, there are speculations about spellbinding being associated with the individual's conscious or oblivious brain.

A few people have accepted that we can associate the oblivious brain through spellbinding throughout the century. Ongoing examinations into the mechanics of spellbinding have indicated that the mind's conscious portion is the most associated one during this psychological state. Nonetheless, the discussion on this is continuous throughout the previous twenty years.

Spellbinding has been characterized in a few stages also. The investigations uncover that these classes depend on the physiological pattern, perspective, and state of being of the subject over the section of years. Additionally, it is likewise founded on the devices utilized for animating the cycle of spellbinding.

Hypnosis has been dealt with more like a spiritualist cycle in the course of the last numerous years. As it may, clinical exploration has demonstrated its advantages as it is nowadays engaged with Trauma treatments that hit patients. Whether one calls it sorcery or medication, if its target stays positive, it is valuable, and its training should proceed.

Hypnosis is a specific mental state with explicit physiological traits, looking like rest just cursorily and set apart by a person working at a degree of mindfulness other than the conventional cognizant state. This state is portrayed by a level of expanded openness and responsiveness in which internal experiential observations are given as much criticalness as is commonly offered distinctly to outside the real world.

What Are the Differences Between Hypnosis on Stage And In Real Life?

Hypnotherapy Vs. Stage Hypnosis

In the realm of spellbinding, there are various kinds of trance specialists and 'subgenres.' However, all things considered, you can classify the employment of entrancing into two unmistakable gatherings: treatment and diversion. When a resident considers entrancing, he thinks about a phase trance inducer, "transforming individuals into chickens" and so forth, or they accept that a trance specialist helps individuals with killing undesirable conduct and accomplish their objectives utilizing spellbinding.

Overall, in case someone hasn't experienced enchanting for both redirection and treatment, they will, as a rule, consider perhaps by the same token. Like this, it is exceptionally normal for new hypnotherapy clients to ask their subconscious authorities quickly before the start of the treatment meeting, "... you're not going to make me a chicken, are you?" Given that hypnotherapy and stage hypnotizing are exceptional, they frequently pack them into one tremendous class of enchanting. Genuinely, stage hypnotizing and hypnotherapy are extraordinary, yet there are likenesses too.

Differentiations

For sure, the essential difference between stage hypnotizing and hypnotherapy is the typical outcome. Stage daze pros need to present a show and give volunteers and the group fun and drawing as expected. Similarly, subconscious stage authorities give suggestions that sole prop up for the range of the show and are dispensed with after the volunteers are 'blended' at the end.

On the other hand, a subconscious authority needs to help clients achieve an individual goal, be it more confidence, halting smoking, resting better, shedding pounds, or various things a client may need to go after. The daze inducer gives a proposition intended to remain past the gathering ('post-entrancing suggestions'), so the client experiences a drawn-out change in various pieces of their life.

This way, one's for redirection, and the spellbinding proposals are temporary. The other is for long stretch personal change and improvement.

Is That the Same?

Surely, the aftereffects of hypnotherapy and stage enchanting are profoundly exceptional, yet countless the systems and approaches used can be on a very basic level equivalent to, if not indistinct. For instance, both stage daze authorities and subconscious pros use 'spellbinding acknowledgments' to entrance their clients/volunteers.

These can be "snappy selections" or "all the more moderate reformist acknowledgments," and the stage daze inducer or the subconscious expert can uphold the two philosophies. Hypnotizing is enchanting, whether or not it is used for redirection or treatment; the state of fascinating is the same. A couple of individuals have all the earmarks of being essentially enchanted than others, yet this is ordinarily a consequence of their receptivity to a hypnotizing proposition rather than the specific strategies used.

Regarding receptivity, suggestibility, and testing/significance are various resemblances between stage enchanting and hypnotherapy. Subconscious masters benefit by knowing how suggestible a volunteer or client is, as it can contact what the trance inducer taught them to do or what likely won't be plausible for said individual.

A stage daze inducer uses suggestibility testing to pick their volunteers (requiring only the most open people from the group). Curiously, a subconscious authority may use comparative tests as a 'warm-up' for the customer or figure out which kind of approaches or recommendations to use or avoid during the treatment meeting.

Concerning happens after someone is spellbound (the treatment or the lovely stuff), a comparative technique is used (really, truly). That technique is called 'proposition.' All subconscious masters and daze inducers use contemplations to make and direct their subjects' experiences.

A stage trance specialist gives suggestions for a volunteer to 'imagine that you are clung to the seat' or 'notice that possibly your shoe is a telephone, and it's ringing, so you ought to get it.'

In like manner, a daze authority may give suggestions for a client to 'imagine looking at yourself in a mirror, seeing the overhauled you that you will be or to observe. That is like that old affinity for smoking has recently moved into the past, and now it's essentially something that you used to do already. The glamorous stage proposals are intended to inspire a more physical/outer reaction from the spellbound volunteers (for individuals to watch). Interestingly, the hypnotherapy recommendations are expected to make a more mental/natural reaction inside the customer (to make changes). Toward the day's end, however, they're all still recommendations.

What Are the Advantages of Hypnotizing Someone?

The Benefits of Controlling Other People

When most people want to learn to hypnotize, they imagine people acting ridiculous on command for the amusement of others or someone lying on a couch while a psychotherapist puts them to sleep.

But hypnosis is simply a heightened state of awareness that opens the mind to seeds of suggestion. When you learn to hypnotize and become a skilled covert hypnotist, you'll know how to take advantage of this receptive state of mind.

When you learn to hypnotize, you lead people to believe that they're following your commands of their own free will. You lead them to think that it was their idea to give you that promotion, buy you that pricey piece of jewelry, or have dinner with you.

Because you're speaking directly to their unconscious mind, they don't even realize what's happening. It doesn't have to be on a sidewalk at a state fair or in a therapist's office.

It can be utilizing one of the most powerful forces that exist between two people: Language. It's not just what you say, but how you say it - and it's not only verbal language, it's body language. And people who learn to hypnotize have realized this.

Imagine being able to change your life through the power of hypnosis. Learn to hypnotize, and you learn to get what you want from people who don't even realize what you're doing.

What are your objectives? What are your goals? What kind of hypnotist do you want to be? If you're like most people, you simply want to guide people in the direction you want them to go. And once you learn to hypnotize, you'll be able to do just that!

Human beings only use about 10 percent of their brainpower. When you learn to hypnotize, you take the first steps toward understanding the mind's full strength.

Once you're able to break into the various dimensions of a person's subconscious, you can start a romance, prosper professionally, and improve your quality of life by tackling the elusiveness of one single life ability - control.

In today's busy world, most of us feel like we're losing grasp of our families, relationships, jobs, and sometimes even ourselves. Imagine being able to regain not only self-control but the ability to influence those around you through covert mind control and underground hypnosis.

Techniques of Dark Psychology

Now, the reason why dark psychology techniques are effectively lying in the way they interact with your psyche. The human psyche is structured to filter out stimuli that somehow don't conform to the patterns, beliefs, and values that permeate the psyche. For instance, if you believe in peace, your mind will reject any notion of violence. By the same token, if your mind is centered on greed and avarice, you may place minimal restrictions on schemes aimed at getting money.

However, the subconscious mind, the layer that exists beneath the conscious mind, is unfiltered but equally able to process the stimuli that enter it. This is why the manipulator's true goal is to access your subconscious and implant ideas at that level. When that happens, the chances of ideas and beliefs sticking are very high.

This is why advertising is so repetitive. Think about it. If you only hear an advert once, the chance of you recalling it would be very slim. However, if you hear adverts over and over, there will come the point where your conscious mind will stop putting up a fight. When that occurs, the message can seep through into your subconscious. This is the secret of brand positioning. So, if you think advertising, at least good advertising anyway, is about selling stuff, guess again. Good advertising is all about getting you to think about a brand or a product constantly.

The Door in The Face!

Directly from the experience of door-to-door salespeople, I present the technique of the door... in the face! When we want to obtain a certain result from our interlocutor, we should request that we consider too high and unreasonable: a metaphorical door will undoubtedly follow this request in the face, that is a refusal; at this point, we should immediately follow the real request that we had in mind: compared with the first the new request will appear more modest and reasonable.

This technique bases its effectiveness on the natural tendency of our minds to make comparisons. If we provide the right term of comparison, no request will appear excessive.

This technique works because it arouses in the person a sense of guilt and an idea of concession. In other words, your renunciation will be perceived as a concession, and then, it is a sneaky application of the "reciprocity rule."

Foot in The Door

This tactic is implemented in increments. This begins with the manipulator asking for small favors. Every time the victim complies, the manipulator will ask for increasingly bigger favors until they get what they ultimately want or exhaust their victim. At that point, the manipulator needs to move on to a fresh victim.

Consider this example:

A manipulator wants a large sum of money. Yet, they know they won't get it if they just ask for it. So, they ask for a tiny sum. Then, they pay it back. After, they ask for a bigger sum and then pay it back. They do this as they build up trust capital until one day; they get what they want, never to be heard from again.

This example clarifies why this technique is called put your "foot in the door" and make room with your whole body...

A more rudimentary approach consists of asking multiple people for money with no intention of paying it back. Eventually, they exhaust the people around them. So, they need to move on and find new victims.

In the "foot in the entryway" method, more modest solicitations are approached to pick up consistence with bigger solicitations, while the strategy "entryway in the face" works the other way, where bigger solicitations are asked, with the desire that it will be dismissed, to pick up consistence for more modest solicitations.

"Yes-Set" Technique

The "yes-set" technique consists of asking several questions to the interlocutor, for which he can only agree and answer "yes." This will create light conditioning that will also make him answer yes to your real request. It is a short-term freezing effect that causes the person to enter into a certain response perspective.

4 or 5 harmless questions in the preamble are enough.

For example, you want to watch a specific program on TV, knowing that the choice of your partner will probably be very different:

YOU: It was nice today, huh? It feels good to get some sun!

HIM/HER: Yes, it was.

YOU: Are you watching TV tonight?

HIM/HER: Well, yes, I think so.

YOU: Remember the movie we saw the day before yesterday?

HIM/HER: Yes.

YOU: I liked it. He was practically the main actor, right?

HIM/HER: Yes, he was.

YOU: Do you agree to watch the 1:00 movie tonight? I think it'll be okay.

HIM/HER: Yes, if you want, what is it?

A funny little demonstration of this principle that I'm sure you already know. Ask someone to repeat the word "white" 10 times, and then ask the question, "What is the cow drinking?" The wrong answer will have been conditioned by past repetition.

This technique's mechanism is based on the use of "rhetorical questions" or statements that are true, taken for granted, or otherwise verifiable in the person's direct experience.

In these cases, the person "leading" the report prepares the ground with a series of questions to which the interlocutor will surely answer yes, which is why it is called "Yes-Set."

And in all three cases, some truisms or true and verifiable statements are followed by an "unverifiable statement" called an induction (or command) or a demand taken for granted.

Linguistic Presupposition

Some very insidious communicative maneuvers consist of asking the interlocutor questions to which it is impossible to answer simply with a "YES" or a "NO," but that trigger in the subject of the actions as an answer to a command. For example, if I ask a person if he "can turn off the light, there on his right?" apparently, I am asking if he can do it, but I will get the switch off in practice, which is actually what I wanted.

In other words, through the linguistic form of "embedded commands," you can skillfully camouflage a command into a question, as in the following example: "Do you want to tell me what's bothering you or would you rather wait a while?"

With this sentence, I create in practice an alternative through the construction of more proposals, where I take for granted that in any case, the subject will reveal to me what worries him.

Linguistic-Presupposition is one of the most powerful and easy to use tools to give someone "apparently" a choice and, at the same time, "trap" them inside your idea, almost without any way out.

Bind is a hypnotic technique used to force a choice with words. It is also called the "illusion of alternative."

Let's see some examples:

- "After you go to buy bread, could you come by the newsstand and buy me the paper?"

- "When are you going to take me to the movies?"

- "Have you decided which foreign country to take me to for our anniversary?"

Each of these questions already provides a choice, and the trick is to take for granted a fact that is slightly hidden.

Reverse Psychology

This technique consists of assuming a behavior opposite to the desired one, with the expectation that this "prohibition" will arouse curiosity and therefore induce the person to do what is desired. For instance, when you tell a child not to do something, that is the first thing they do. This type of response persists throughout a person's life.

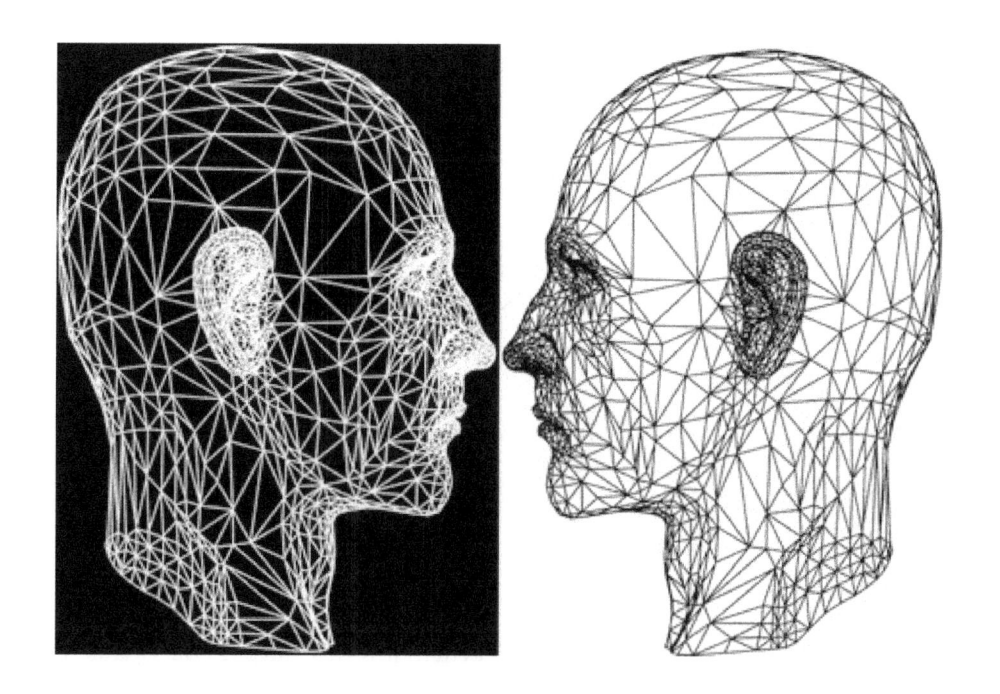

It's a way of getting things done, giving the opposite of the command you want. If I say things like, "don't be offended" "don't worry," I get the opposite effect. I will make my interlocutor stiffen.

Some people are known to be like boomerangs because they refuse to go in the direction, they are sent but take the opposite route. A dark persuader can use this type of behavior because it is a weakness that the victim has. Take an example of a friend who loves to eat junk food at any opportunity they get. The dark persuader knows this and therefore will suggest that they should eat healthy because it will be good for them, knowing that the friend will choose fast food anyway.

When individuals are told that they should not believe one thing or the other, they will pay closer attention.

Consider this situation:

You are looking to force your employees to work overtime without questioning it. However, getting them to log the hours can be challenging as no one is keen on staying beyond their usual shift. So, you really can't do much to convince them to work overtime.

Then, you get an idea: Why not ban overtime? That is, anyone who wants to work overtime cannot do so. The justification behind it is that since no one wants to stay longer hours, there will be no overtime. You could take it a step further and hire temp workers to fill in the extra hours. Now, your regular staff is concerned that others are infringing upon their jobs. In the end, you may get resistance from your usual staff who are now demanding to work overtime to get rid of the temp workers.

In the end, you have successfully manipulated your staff to work overtime. You were able to play with their sense of security by banning overtime and then bringing other workers to cover the hours they wouldn't.

A convention playbook would have sought to incentivize workers to be more willing to stay longer hours. But this would have meant paying more or offering greater benefits. In the end, your manipulation attempts were successful without conceding any additional benefits.

Negative Hidden Commands

A negative hidden command is a specific linguistic model of reverse psychology in which instruction is formulated negatively so that it is perceived by the unconscious mind, bypassing the "critical guardian" of our interlocutor.

An interesting aspect of the unconscious mind is that it does not understand negation than the conscious one. This happens because our mind works by images and because there is no mental representation of the word "NOT." Therefore, the unconscious does not perceive it. In other words, our brain cannot deny experiences related to the senses without first visualizing them.

Generally, in Guerrilla Marketing, NLP, the psychology of communication, and neuro-marketing, two examples are given below to explain this concept.

1.Read the following sentence and do what it says: "Don't think of a pink elephant."

What were you thinking? Almost certainly a pink elephant, even though you were asked not to.

2. Now I ask you not to think of a yellow lemon. Think about what you want, but don't think of a yellow lemon. Don't think of a big, juicy yellow lemon, its intense aroma, its sour taste. Don't think about cutting the yellow lemon in two, squeezing half of it in your mouth, and drinking its sour juice.

CONCLUSION

Thank you for reading all this book!

The fact that you were willing to read this book to the end shows your dedication and desire to gain knowledge on the subject of manipulation. If you have been listening, you have realized that dark psychology can affect anyone. Whether you are young or old, you must equip yourself with some knowledge on the subject of dark psychology.

You have already taken a step towards your improvement.
Best wishes!

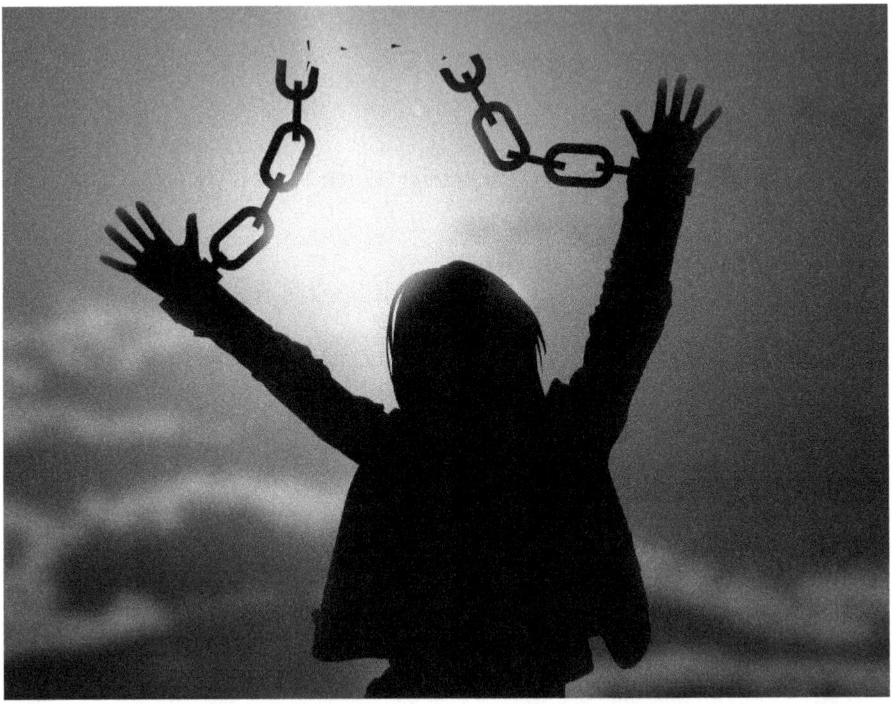

CPSIA information can be obtained
at www.ICGtesting.com
Printed in the USA
BVHW041517190321
602997BV00010B/610

9 781802 088199